The
of the
North Star

by Emily Bluestone
Illustrated by Vicki Bradley

Editorial Offices: Glenview, Illinois • Parsippany, New Jersey • New York, New York
Sales Offices: Needham, Massachusetts • Duluth, Georgia • Glenview, Illinois
Coppell, Texas • Sacramento, California • Mesa, Arizona

stars

How did the North Star get into the sky? The Paiute (pi YOOT) Indians imagined this story about the North Star.

Look overhead at the sky at night. The sky is filled with stars. Did you know that stars move? A long, long time ago, the Paiute Indians say, the People of the Sky made trails through the heavens. The stars follow these trails as they move in the sky.

Each night almost every star is in a different place. Only the North Star stays in the same place. This is its story.

Paiute: Native American tribe living in parts of California, Nevada, Utah, Arizona, and Oregon

mountain

A long time ago, a mountain sheep called Na-gah lived on earth. His father's name was Shinoh. Na-gah and Shinoh belonged to the People of the Sky.

Na-gah was the strongest and bravest of all the mountain sheep. He liked to climb the tallest mountains. Shinoh was very proud of his son.

One day, Na-gah traveled very far. He saw a tall, rocky mountain. Na-gah wanted to climb this mountain. He was sure that he could do it. He wanted his father to be proud of him.

Na-gah walked around the mountain many times. He could not find a trail to go to the top. How could he reach the top?

I must find a way up, he thought. *My father will be proud of me if I climb this mountain.*

At last he found a narrow crack in a rock. Na-gah squeezed through the crack and went inside the mountain. It was very dark. Na-gah could not see anything.

But then he found a path that went up a steep hill. *So,* thought Na-gah, *the path up the mountain is inside the mountain. I can do this.* He started up the hill.

mountain sheep

Na-gah walked and walked. Soon the path became very rocky. Na-gah stepped lightly on the rocks, but some of them crashed to the bottom.

Maybe I should turn back, Na-gah thought. But when he looked down, he saw that

rocks

the falling rocks had blocked the path. He could not go back down. Na-gah had to keep climbing up, up, up.

Na-gah began to slip on the rocks. His body hurt, and he began to lose courage. He had never been afraid in his life, but now he was afraid.

Na-gah had great courage, but he was getting too tired to go on. Just when he thought he could not go another step, he looked up and saw a crack of light. *At last!* Na-gah thought. *I have reached the top!* He found new strength and kept moving up.

Finally, Na-gah squeezed through the rocks and was back on the outside of the mountain. He looked around. He had reached the very top!

"I made it!" Na-gah shouted. "I am at the top! My father will be so proud."

mountaintop

Na-gah looked around again. His joy turned to sadness. He realized that he could not go down the mountain. He would have to live on this mountaintop forever.

Then Na-gah heard his father calling. His father was walking across the sky. "Na-gah! Na-gah!" Shinoh shouted. He looked everywhere but could not see his son.

"Look, Father!" Na-gah shouted. "I am here at the top of the tallest mountain!"

realized: understood

Shinoh looked proudly at his son. He was happy Na-gah had climbed the tallest mountain. But then he realized that there was no way down! Shinoh felt sad. "There is my son," he said. "He can never come down from the mountain. But I will do something special for him. I will turn him into a star to shine forever in the sky."

So Shinoh turned Na-gah into the North Star. All the other stars move across the heavens. But the North Star never moves. It is always in the same place.

And that is how Na-gah became the North Star—how the North Star began.